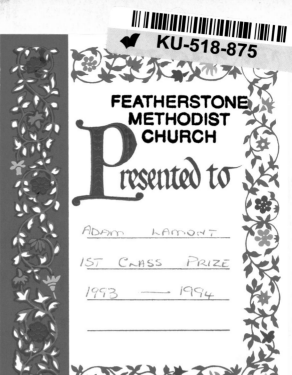

**FEATHERSTONE
METHODIST
CHURCH**

Presented to

ADAM LAMONT

1ST CLASS PRIZE

1993 — 1994

CHRISTIAN ART LTD, EXETER, 0392 77277

Can you find
all of these objects
in this book?
You will have to look
very hard.

Telling The Time, Animal Babies, Wonderful Wheels & Pets
written by Anne McKie.

My First Picture Book of Numbers, My First Rhyming ABC
written by Brian Miles. Text ©1985 Brian Miles.

Illustrated by Ken McKie.

Published by
GRANDREAMS LIMITED
Jadwin House, 205/211 Kentish Town Road, London, NW5 2JU.

Printed in Czech Republic.

LO5

MY BIG BOOK OF
LEARNING

This book belongs to:

....

....

....

Age...........................

FEEDING TIMES

Sea Lions		12:00
Penguins		12:30
Children		13:00
Lions and Tigers		13:30

CONTENTS

my first picture book of numbers

this is 1~one

one currant bun

1 2 3 4 5 6 7 8 9 10

this is 2~two

two red shoes

1 **2** 3 4 5 6 7 8 9 10

this is 3~three

three birds in a tree

1 2 **3** 4 5 6 7 8 9 10

this is 4~four

four windows in the door

1 2 3 **4** 5 6 7 8 9 10

this is 5~five

**five bees round
the hive**

1 2 3 4 5 6 7 8 9 10

this is 6~six

six fluffy chicks

1 2 3 4 5 6 7 8 9 10

this is 7~seven

there are seven days in a week

1 2 3 4 5 6 **7** 8 9 10

A B C 1 2 3 4 5 6

this is 8~eight

eight bars in the gate

1 2 3 4 5 6 7 8 9 10

A B C 1 2 3 a b c 4 5 6

this is 9~nine

nine trees in a line

A B C 1 2 3 4 5 6

this is 10~ten

ten chicks and a hen

1 2 3 4 5 6 7 8 9 10

this is 11~eleven

eleven musical instruments

11 12 13 14 15 16 17 18 19 20

this is 12~twelve

there are twelve months
in a year

January	July
February	August
March	September
April	October
May	November
June	December

11 12 13 14 15 16 17 18 19 20

A B C 1 2 3 4 5 6

this is 13~thirteen

can you count thirteen ducks on the pond?

11 12 13 14 15 16 17 18 19 20

this is 14~fourteen

here are fourteen children

four in this row-4

and ten in this row-10

4+10=14

11 12 13 14 15 16 17 18 19 20

this is 15~fifteen

here are fifteen cats

eight in this row-8

and seven in this row-7

8+7=15

11 12 13 14 **15** 16 17 18 19 20

this is 16~sixteen

here are sixteen lollies

ten in this row–10

and six in this row–6

10+6=16

11 12 13 14 15 16 17 18 19 20

this is 17~seventeen

here are seventeen flowers

eight in this row-8

and nine in this row-9

8+9=17

11 12 13 14 15 16 17 18 19 20

this is 18~eighteen

here are eighteen socks

nine on this line-9

and nine on this line-9

9+9=18

11 12 13 14 15 16 17 **18** 19 20

this is 19~nineteen

here are nineteen pencils

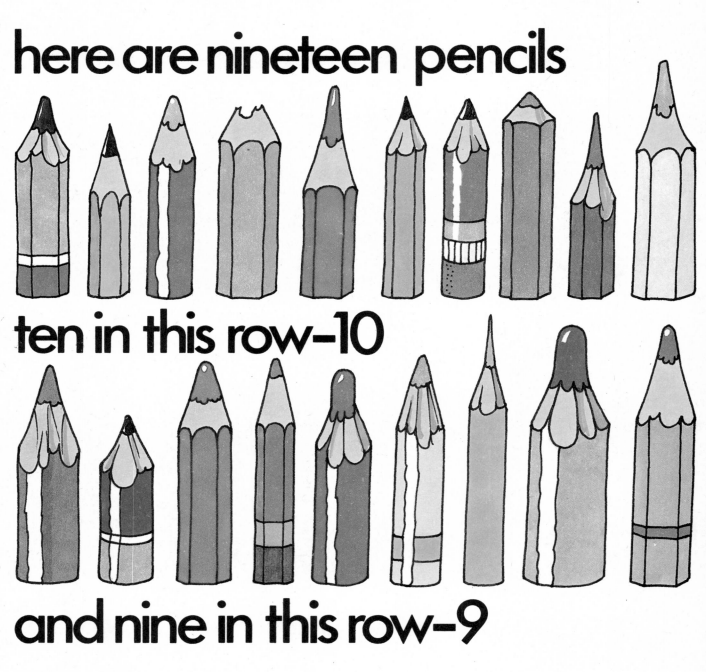

ten in this row–10

and nine in this row–9

10+9=19

11 12 13 14 15 16 17 18 19 20

this is 20~twenty

here are twenty bottles

ten in this row–10

and ten in this row

10+10=20

11 12 13 14 15 16 17 18 19 20

this is 30~thirty

thirty is three tens,
can you count 30 candles
on the cake?

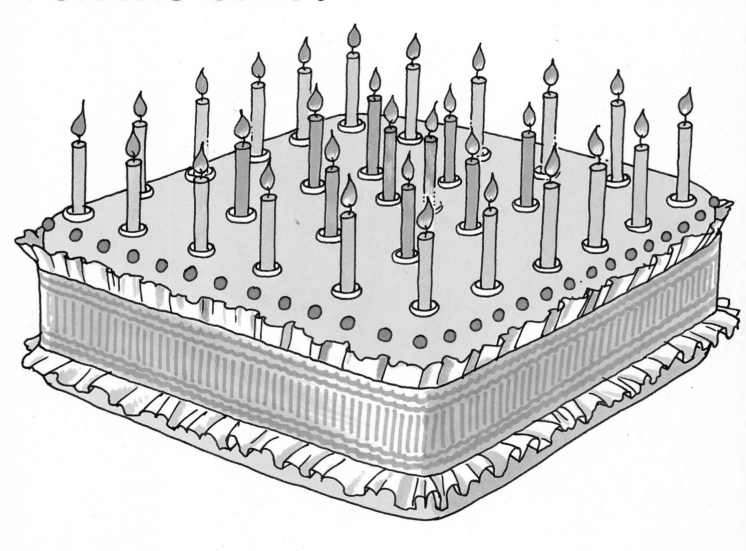

10   20   30   40   50

this is 40~forty

forty is four tens,
can you count 40 apples
on this tree?

60   70   80   90   100

this is 50 ~ fifty

fifty is five tens,
can you count 50
stones in the river?

10   20   30   40   50

this is 60~sixty

sixty is six tens,
can you count 60 minutes
on the clock?

60   70   80   90   100

ABC123⌚abc456

this is 70~seventy

seventy is seven tens,
can you add up all the fruit
to make 70?

10 🍎🍎🍎🍎🍎🍎🍎🍎🍎🍎

10 🍊🍊🍊🍊🍊🍊🍊🍊🍊🍊

10 🍌🍌🍌🍌🍌🍌🍌🍌🍌🍌

10 🍋🍋🍋🍋🍋🍋🍋🍋🍋🍋

10 🍐🍐🍐🍐🍐🍐🍐🍐🍐🍐

10 🫐🫐🫐🫐🫐🫐🫐🫐🫐🫐

10 🍓🍓🍓🍓🍓🍓🍓🍓🍓🍓

10   20   30   40   50

this is 80~eighty

eighty is eight tens,
can you add up all the objects
to make 80?

10
10
10
10
10
10
10
10

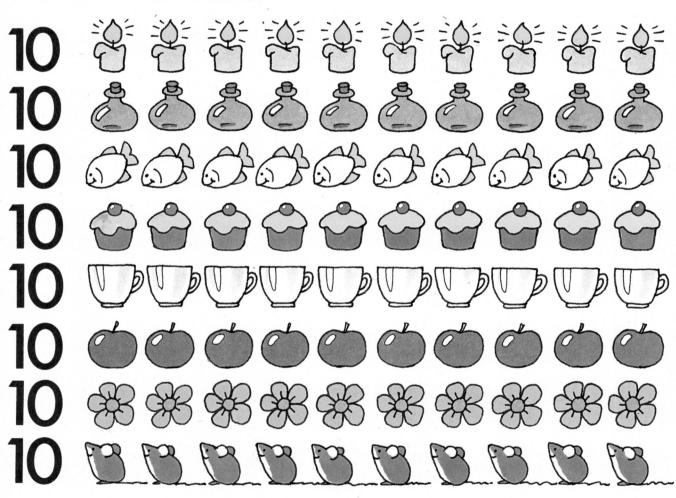

60 70 80 90 100

this is 90~ninety

ninety is nine tens,
can you add up all the objects
to make 90?

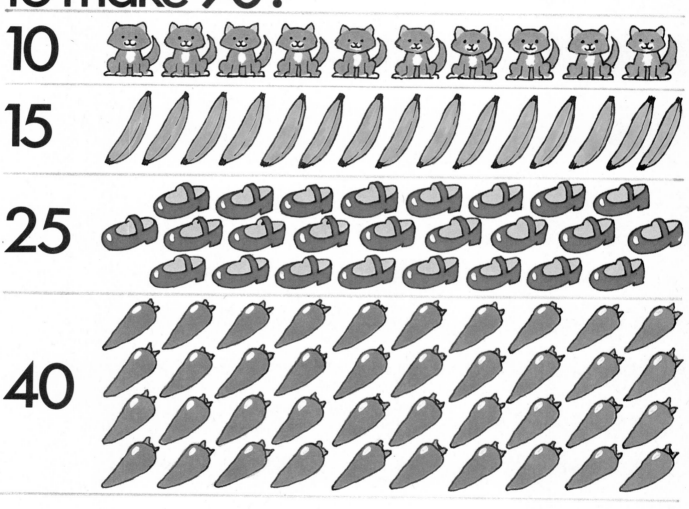

10

15

25

40

10   20   30   40   50

this is 100~hundred

one hundred is ten tens,
can you add up these numbers
to make 100?

ten _____ 10
fifteen _____ 15
twenty _____ 20
twenty five _____ 25
thirty _____ 30
_____
_____

well done!

60   70   80   90   100

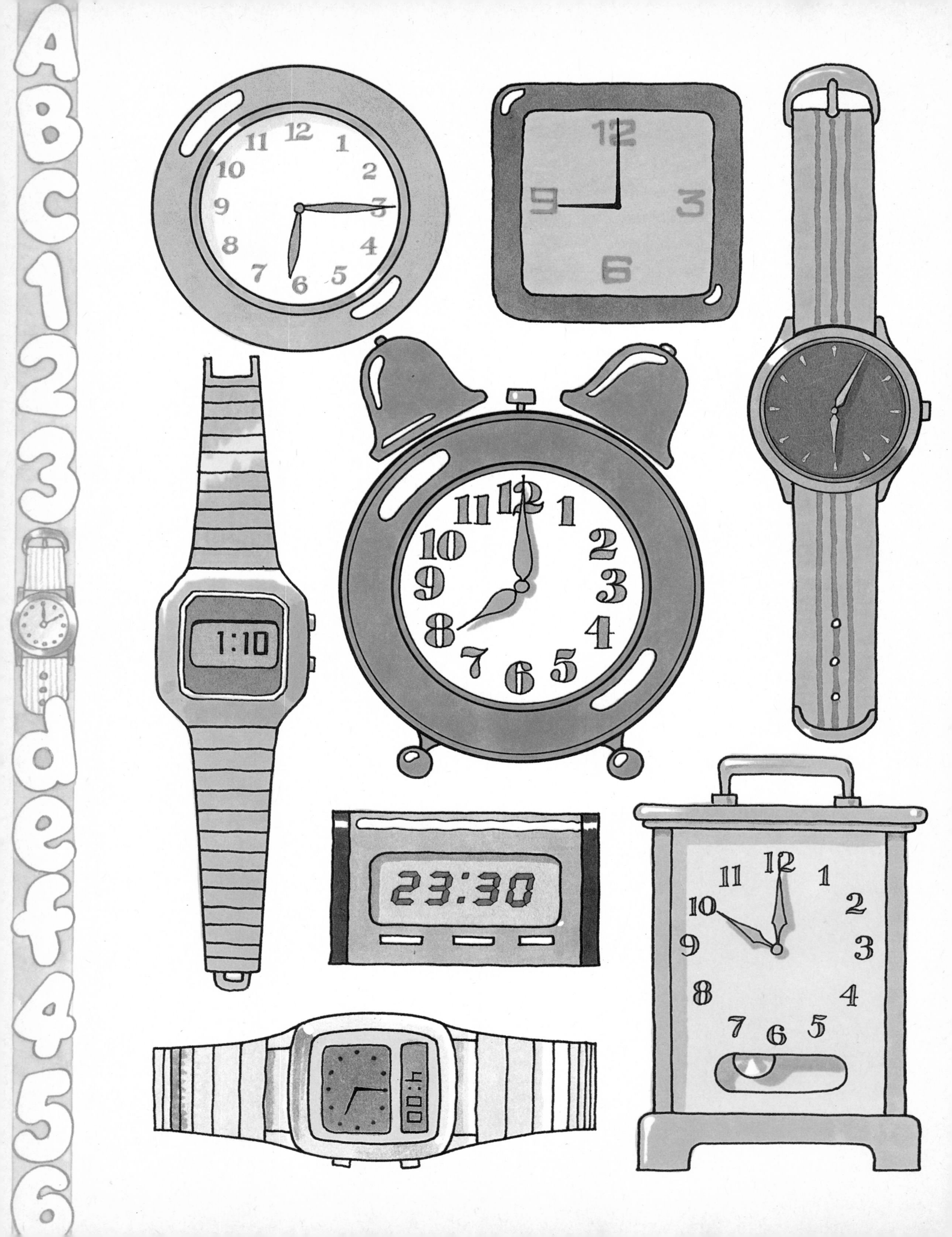
1:10
23:30

my first book of

TELLING THE TIME

On the clock face the long hand points to the minutes, the short hand points to the hour. Sometimes on clocks and watches there is another hand which goes round the face very quickly, it is called the second hand.

There are 60 seconds in a minute.
A second is as quick as a wink.

There are 60 minutes in an hour.

There are two types of clock, one with a face and hands, and one that just has numbers called digits. Some digital clocks show 12 hours, others show the full 24 hours in a day.

This is 2 o'clock in the afternoon on a 12 hour clock.

This is the same time on a 24 hour clock.

These clocks show all 24 hours in a day.
The time from 12 midnight to 12 noon is called
'A.M.'. From noon to midnight is called 'P.M.'.

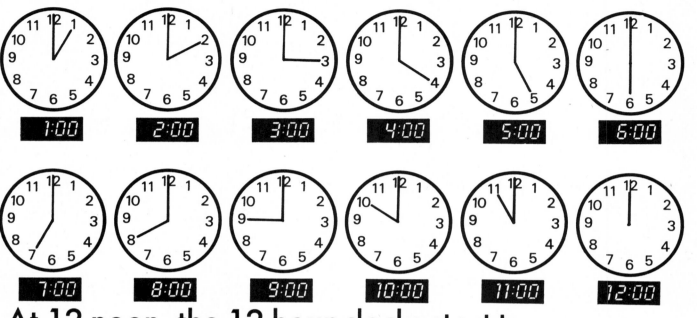

At 12 noon, the 12 hour clocks start to go
round again. The 24 hour clocks just go on
adding up to 24.

At 12 midnight a new day begins, and all the
clocks start again.

Here is a story about an exciting day out. Learn about time from the little clocks in each picture.

The twins are fast asleep. It is 7 o'clock.

7:00

Here comes the milkman. It is 7.15, a quarter past seven.

7:15

Here comes the postman with the letters and a parcel. It is 7.30, half past seven.

7:30

Mother calls: "Get up, it's late, it is 8 o'clock. We are going out today."

The twins jump out of bed and run to the bathroom to get washed.

Hurry up twins, get dressed straight away. Pull on your socks, put on your shoes, it is 8.15, a quarter past eight.

Breakfast is on the table ready to eat. It is 8.30, half past eight.

"Grab your coats, I will lock the door. The bus will be here at 9 o'clock," says mother.

They get to the bus stop out of breath. Here comes the bus, right on time.

"Where are we going?" ask the twins. Mother says: "Wait and see." The bus stops at the railway station at 9.15, a quarter past nine.

The train arrives at 9.30, half past nine by the station clock. Climb aboard, and off we go.

The train speeds on through the countryside, past woods and fields and over bridges. Half an hour goes by. It is now 10 o'clock.

10:00

At last the train stops at a little station and everyone gets off.

The ticket collector has a big watch that says 10.15, a quarter past ten.

The twins and their mother leave the station and start walking down the lane.

It was a lovely walk down the lanes, through a village, and past a church with a clock that said 10.45, a quarter to eleven.

10:45

"Here we are at last," says mother. It is a park with lots of animals. "We open at 11 o'clock," says the man at the gate, "you're just on time."

11:00

ANIMAL LAND

First they see a hippo.

Then a zebra with lots of stripes.

They make friends with a monkey...

...but not with the camel.

Then it was 11.45, a quarter to twelve. "Come on," says mother, "there's something I want you to see."

The keeper is feeding the
sea lions at 12 o'clock.

12:00

At 12.30, half past twelve, he feeds
the penguins with fish from a
bucket, and the twins help him.

12:30

"Look! It's 1 o'clock," says mother. "It's our feeding time now. We will have a picnic at that table over there."

It is afternoon. The 24 hour clock now says 13.00, the thirteenth hour of the day.

Mother says: "It is 1.30, half past one. I will sit here and you can look around for an hour by yourselves."

First the twins go to see the parrots and the other lovely birds.

At 2 o'clock they go to Pets Corner
to play with the baby animals.

2:00   14:00

When they get back to mother, she says: "You are just in time to see the dolphins at 2.30, half past two."

"Oh dear," say the twins, looking at their watches. "It is 3 o'clock and there is still so much to see."

They see a big brown bear.

A tiger that growls at them.

And a lion that is fast asleep.

3:45   15:45

They see a giraffe, as tall as a house...

...and a big bad tempered rhino.

"Have we time to see the snakes and the crocodiles?" ask the twins. "Yes," says mother. "If we are finished by 5 o'clock.

5:00   17:00

"You two must be hungry," says mother.
"We have time for a quick snack before
we leave for home."

When everyone has finished eating,
the clock says 5.30, half past five.

"Now we must hurry to the gates," says mother. "The park closes at 6 o'clock."

"Goodbye," says the man at the gate. "I hope you have enjoyed your visit."

6:00   18:00

They get back to the station at 6.45, a quarter to seven. Mother says: "We have to wait 15 minutes for the 7 o'clock train."

6:45   18:45

Here it comes, right on time.

7:00   19:00

After their journey by train and bus they arrive home at 8 o'clock just as it is getting dark.

The twins go straight upstairs to get washed and ready for bed.

Mother brought them a hot drink. "You must be tired," she says. "It is 8.30, half past eight."

8:30   20:30

By 9 o'clock they are both fast asleep. It has been a long busy day!

9:00   21:00

The twins are asleep, but the clocks go on counting the time up to 12 o'clock midnight.

10:00 **22:00**   **11:00** **23:00**   **12:00** **24:00**

Can you fill in the missing times from these clocks?

7:30   :   8:45   :

10:00   :   11:30   :

12:15   :   3:00   4:45

my first rhyming picture abc

A a

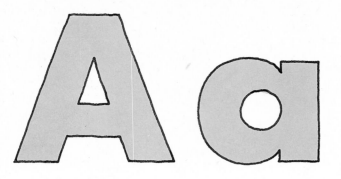

a is for apples
some green, some red

a is for aeroplane
that flies overhead

a is for apricot
that grows on a tree

a is for adding
one, two, three

B b

b is for baker
who bakes crusty bread

b is for blanket
that covers your bed

b is for beaker
for drinking your tea

b is for binoculars
for miles you can see

C c

C is for cat
with its whiskers long

C is for cart
pulled by a horse so strong

C is for carrot
crunchy and sweet

C is for cars
that you see in the street

D d

d is for dancing
so light on your feet

d is for drinking
orange juice so sweet

d is for dog
wagging his tail

d is for dinghy
with a bright blue sail

E e

e is for eggs
see the chicks that hatch out

e is for excitement
when we all laugh and shout

e is for elephant
so gentle but strong

e is for ending
the show with a song

F f

f is for farm
with fresh milk and cheese

f is for fingers
the toothpaste to squeeze

f is for fan
a cool breeze to make

f is for fish
that swim in the lake

ABC 123 4 5 6

G g

g is for grapes
some green, some black

g is for garbage
that's put in a sack

g is for garden
where flowers do grow

g is for gumboots
to wear in the snow

H h

h is for hedgehog
who cleans up the garden

h is for hiccup
I beg your pardon!

h is for hymn
that is sung in a church

h is for hen
asleep on her perch

I i

i is for island
surrounded by sea

i is for iguana
a lizard you see

The Sun

i is for inn
a welcoming sight

i is for ivory
so smooth and so white

J j

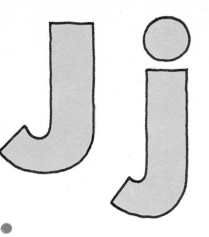

j is for jug
full of water so cool

j is for jumping
into the pool

j is for jam
to spread on your bread

STRAWBERRY JAM

j is for jet
that roars overhead

K k

k is for king
so stately and tall

k is for kitten
who plays with the ball

k is for kitchen
where cooking is done

k is for keeping
a secret, it's fun

L l

l is for lion
so noble and strong

l is for the lark
and merry birdsong

l is for leopard
known for his spots

l is for lemon
to squeeze lots and lots

M m

m is for mouse
who lives in a barn

m is for minstrel
who sings his own yarn

m is for mask
that hides your face

25miles

m is for marathon
a very long race

N n

n is for nurse
so patient with care

n is for nightingale
with its song so rare

n is for nut
so crunchy to eat

n is for navy
and ships in the fleet

O is for orange
as round as a ball

O is for ostrich
with its neck so tall

O is for oblong
longer than a square

O is for orchid
a flower so rare

P p

p is for parrot
a beautiful bird

p is for pasture
and grazing a herd

p is for parachute
that floats to the ground

p is for pumpkin
oval or round

Q q

ABC123@def456

q is for quack
it's the way a duck talks

q is for queen
who smiles as she walks

q is for quilt
so warm yet so light

q is for quail
in migratory flight

R r

r is for robin
with its bright red breast

r is for rook
high in his nest

r is for roses
that grow down the lane

r is for rainbow
after the rain

ABC123456

S s

S is for sparrow
to the garden he comes

S is for starling
looking for crumbs

S is for snow
cold, crisp and white

S is for stars
that shine in the night

ABC
123
456

T t

t is for target
at which we take aim

t is for teddybear
he's good for a game

t is for ticket
to ride on the train

t is for tea-time
it's jelly again!

U u

U is for universe
the planets and stars

U is for Uranus
a planet, like Mars

U is for uniforms
the guards in a row

U is for under
the arches we go!

V v

V is for vine
heavy with fruit

V is for valet
preparing a suit

V is for vikings
who sailed the high seas

V is for vegetables
potatoes, parsnips and peas

Ww

W is for water
we use to make tea

W is for whale
that swims in the sea

W is for the willow
that grows by the stream

W is for waking
from a beautiful dream

X x

X is for x-rays
used in hospitals you know
they can see through you
from your head to your toe

X is for xylophone
an instrument to play

X is for ten
the old roman way

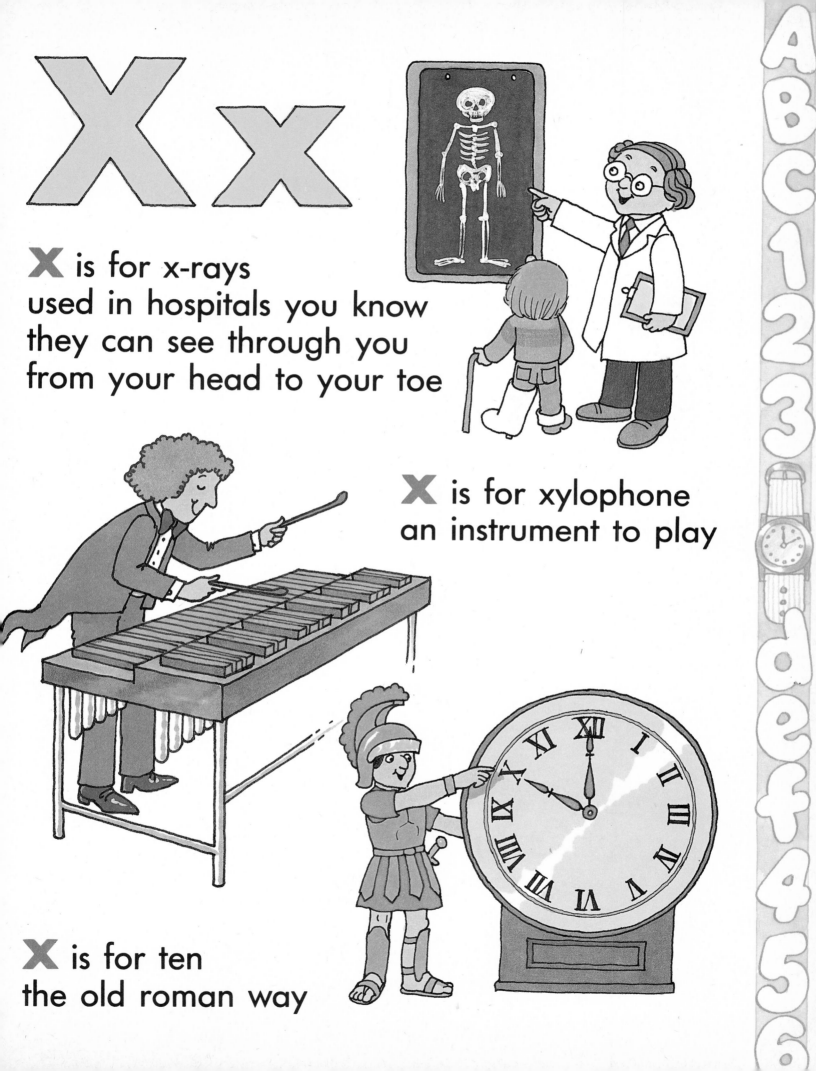

Y y

y is for yellow
and daffodils so pale

y is for yacht
under full sail

y is for yeast
that helps make bread dough

y is for yearling
a young horse you know

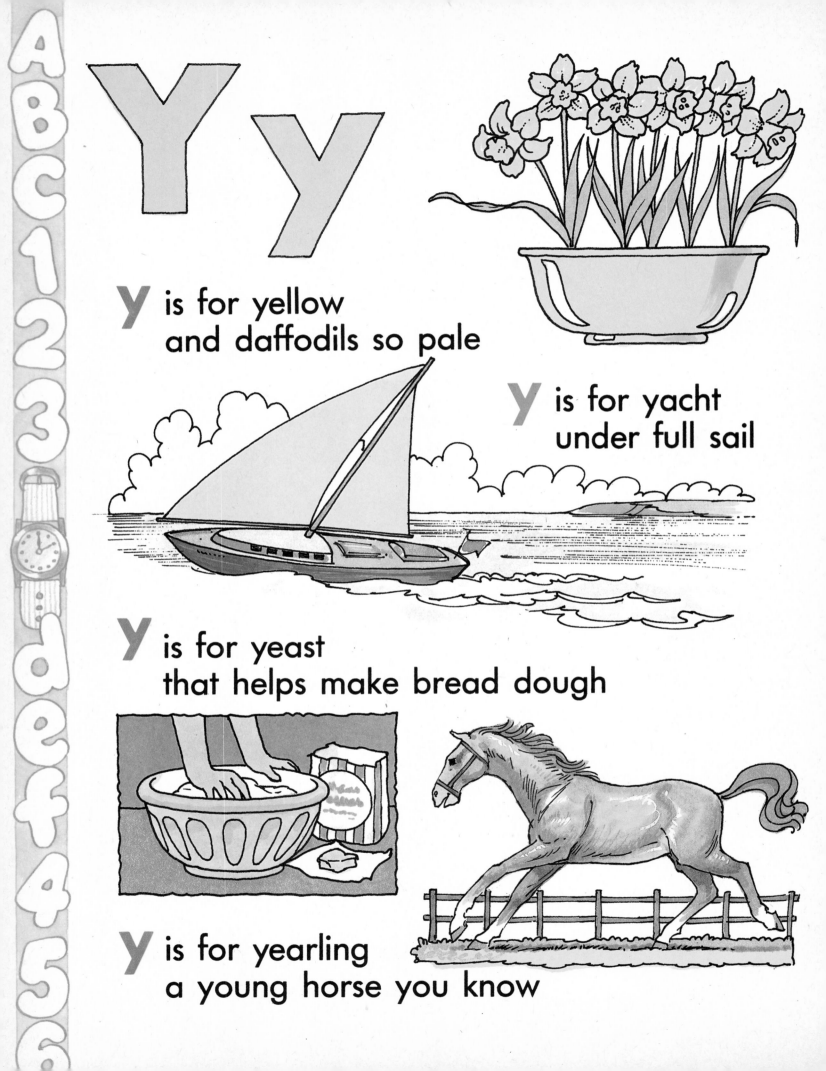

Zz

Z is for zebras
with their black and white coats

Z is for zither
playing musical notes

Z is for zoo
and the animals there

Z is for zig-zag
in a car beware

My first book of
Animal Babies

Everyone loves baby animals.
In this book you will find all
kinds of babies from all around
the world.

If you visit a farm or a pets corner in
the zoo you can often hold the young
animals. Sometimes you can also help to
feed them.

Baby animals in the wild
love to play, but their parents
can be dangerous.
    We have to see wild animals
in zoos or on nature films.

Remember, don't take
any baby animal away, its
mother will be close by.

Here are some of the babies that you can see on a farm.

How many chicks do the hen and the cockerel have?

You can make friends with all the baby animals on a farm

Here comes the farmer with some food for the calf.

How many ducklings are going for a swim?

especially these hungry little pigs.

Here is the farmer's wife with a baby donkey
and a very young horse. They are both called foals.

Someone has left the gate open. Can you
count the lambs that have got out?

Two little goats play in the field.
They are called kids.

Three little goslings
going for a walk with
mother goose and
father gander.

When you visit the countryside and walk through the fields and woods, you may spot lots of animals and their babies...if you are quiet.

Foxes

Red Deer

Hedgehogs

Rabbits

Badgers

Baby animals and their parents.

Human family

Reindeer

Porcupines

Leopards

Cattle

Swans

Sheep

Kangaroos

In the zoo some baby animals are easy to handle.

Zebra

Llama

Others are more lively.

Chimps

These baby animals are soft and furry.

Koala

Raccoon

Giant Panda

Some baby animals are very big and heavy.

Giraffe

Elephant

Hippo

Rhino

Other baby animals are very small.

Tortoises

Squirrels

Skunks

Mice

Quail chicks

These baby animals live in very cold countries.

Seals

Polar bears

Penguins

These baby animals live in very hot countries.

Kangaroo

Camel

Lion

Wild pigs

Some baby animals look very soft and cuddly when they are babies, but they grow up to be very dangerous in the wild.

Tiger

Lions

Crocodiles

Wolves

Grizzly bears

Do you have a favourite soft toy shaped like a baby animal?

This little bear likes his Teddy bear.

MILK

My first book of
Wonderful
WHEELS

A wheel is round like an `O'.
Look at the wheels around this picture.

Wheels go round and round.
This makes things easier to push,
and pull.

These children are having
great fun with wheels.

Here are some wheels for babies. They make prams and buggies easy to push.

SWINGS

LAKE

Here is a wonderful toy with lots of wheels.

Can you count them?

Pedal cart

BMX bike

Trike

Tractor and trailer

Do you have any toys like this?

Police pedal car

Tractor and bucket

Remote control truck

How many wheels can you count?
Don't forget the steering wheels.

1 My bike has one wheel.
It is very hard to stay on!

2 My bike has two wheels.
I can ride fast.

3 My bike has three wheels.
It is very easy to ride.

But my bike is a motorbike.
It is very fast...and very noisy!

This is a very old car.

This is a very new car.

This is a racing car.

ZIP

This is a car transporter, it delivers new cars to garages.

Taxi!

This car can go over rough country.

These wheels bring us things we like.

The drivers are having to change a wheel...

Can you tell which wheel goes where?

Look at the huge wheels on these trucks.

Earth moving truck

Four wheel drive

Low loader

Do you have any toy trucks like these?

Tipper truck

Wheels take us from place to place.

This is an old steam train.

This is a new electric train.

Lots of people can travel in a train or a coach.

This coach is taking people on holiday.

Oh dear, the school bus has a flat tyre, but the driver has a spare.

SCHOOL BUS

These wheels bring us help when we are in trouble or danger.

The ambulance takes people to hospital.

The motorcycle policeman
can go very fast to where
he is needed.

Here is the fire engine.
The fire will soon be put out.

MILK

Look at all these wheels.
Big wheels, little wheels, fast wheels,
slow wheels, lots and lots of

WONDERFUL WHEELS

Up in the air

"Hello, I am a bird and I can fly. Most birds and some insects can fly because they have wings. Look up in the air and see how many creatures you can see flying around."

On warm, sunny days you can find lots of flying insects and birds.

The bat and the owl can fly in the dark.

Ducks can fly...
and swim

" Here are some very colourful kites. On a breezy day you can have great fun flying a kite up in the air."

This is a very windy day.
Look what gets blown
up in the air.

Do you have any toys that will fly up in the air? Here is a paper dart that is easy to make.

You will need a flat sheet of paper about the size of this page.

Crease it down the middle.

1

Fold two corners.

2

And fold again.

3

4

Fold it
like this.

5

Fold the
wings down.

6

Fold down
a 1cm strip.

Your paper dart is now ready to fly.
Throw it gently and see how far it can go.
(Look for the paper darts flying around in this book.)

This is a boomerang, throw it and it will come back to you.

Bows and arrows
are great fun, but you
must be careful.

"I'm safer on the ground!"

"If you cannot fly like me, see how high you can jump up in the air."

Can you jump as high as a kangaroo?

Or hop as fast as a rabbit?

Or leap as far as a frog?

This is a
pole vaulter.

He can jump really high.

These children can bounce high.

But not as high as the clown on the trampoline.

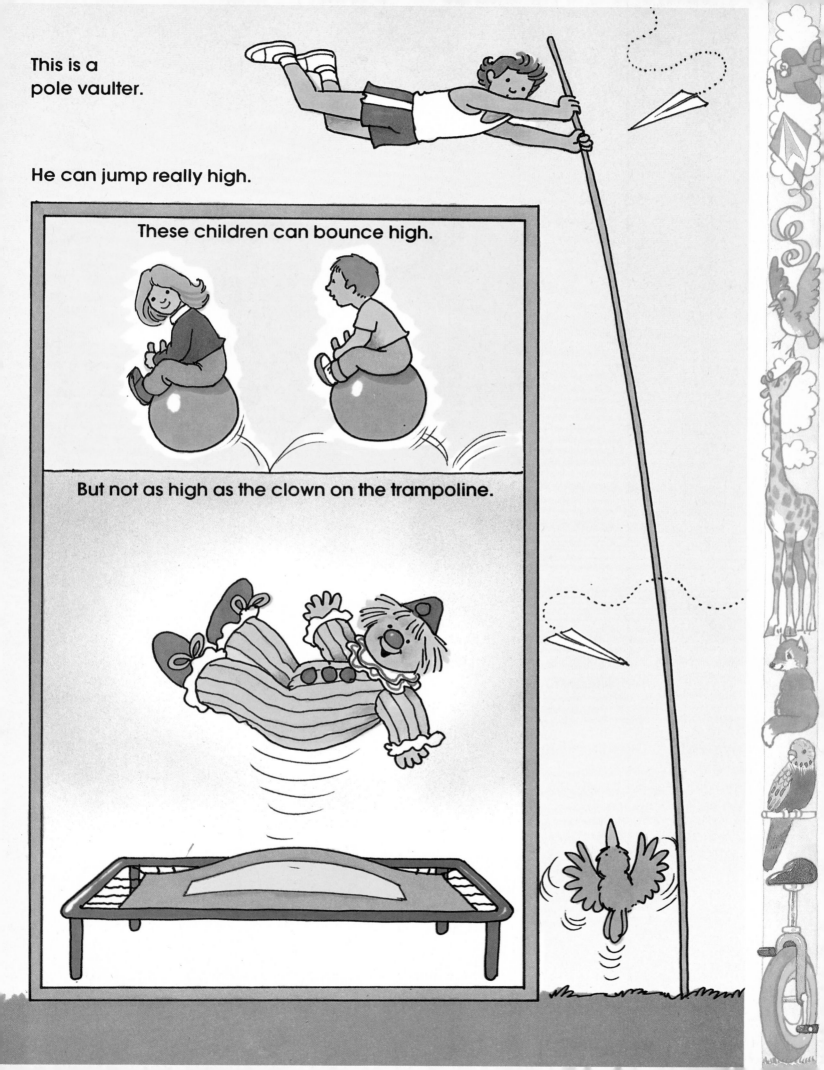

Here are some people who work high up in the air. They have to be careful not to fall.

Harry is a steeplejack. He works on very tall buildings.

Tony and Angela are circus trapeze artistes.

This is Jo, she is a house painter.

This is Brian, he is a painter too.

Pete and Barry clean windows on tall office buildings.

SHINY BRIGHT COMPANY

Eric fits television aerials.

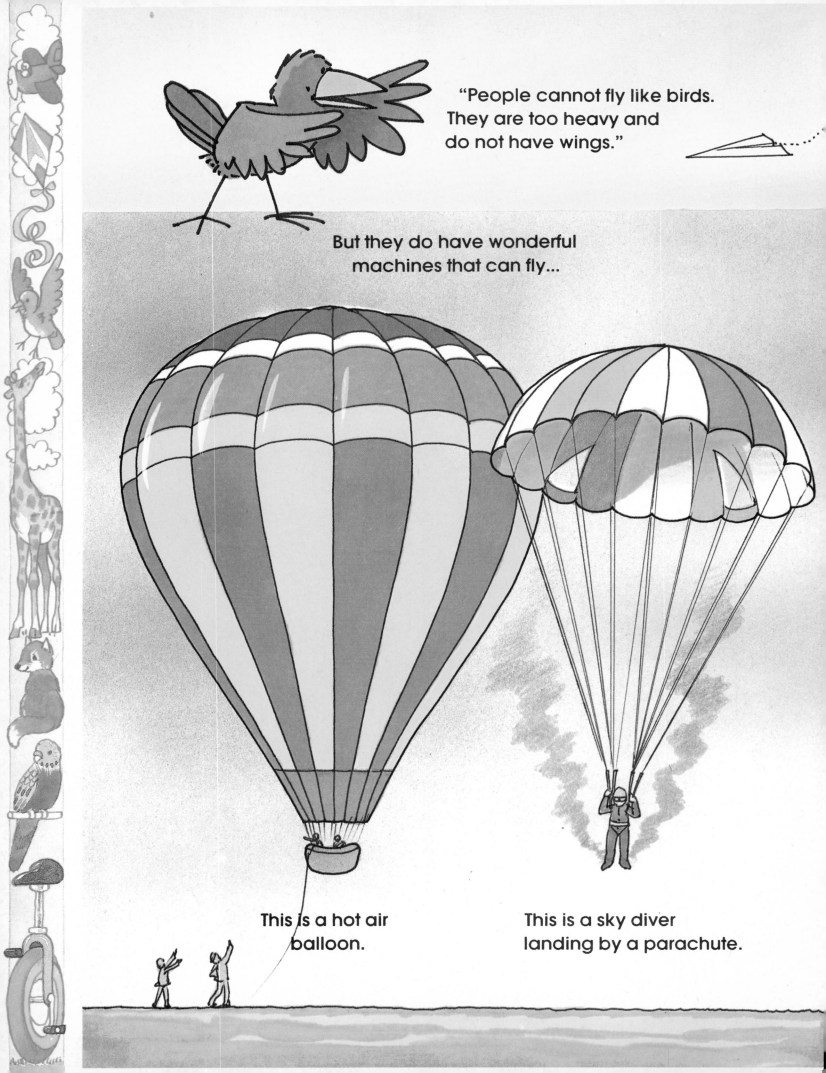

"People cannot fly like birds.
They are too heavy and
do not have wings."

But they do have wonderful
machines that can fly...

This is a hot air
balloon.

This is a sky diver
landing by a parachute.

A hang glider.
The pilot steers by moving
his body from side to side.

A Microlight is a very light
aircraft, almost a hang glider
with an engine.

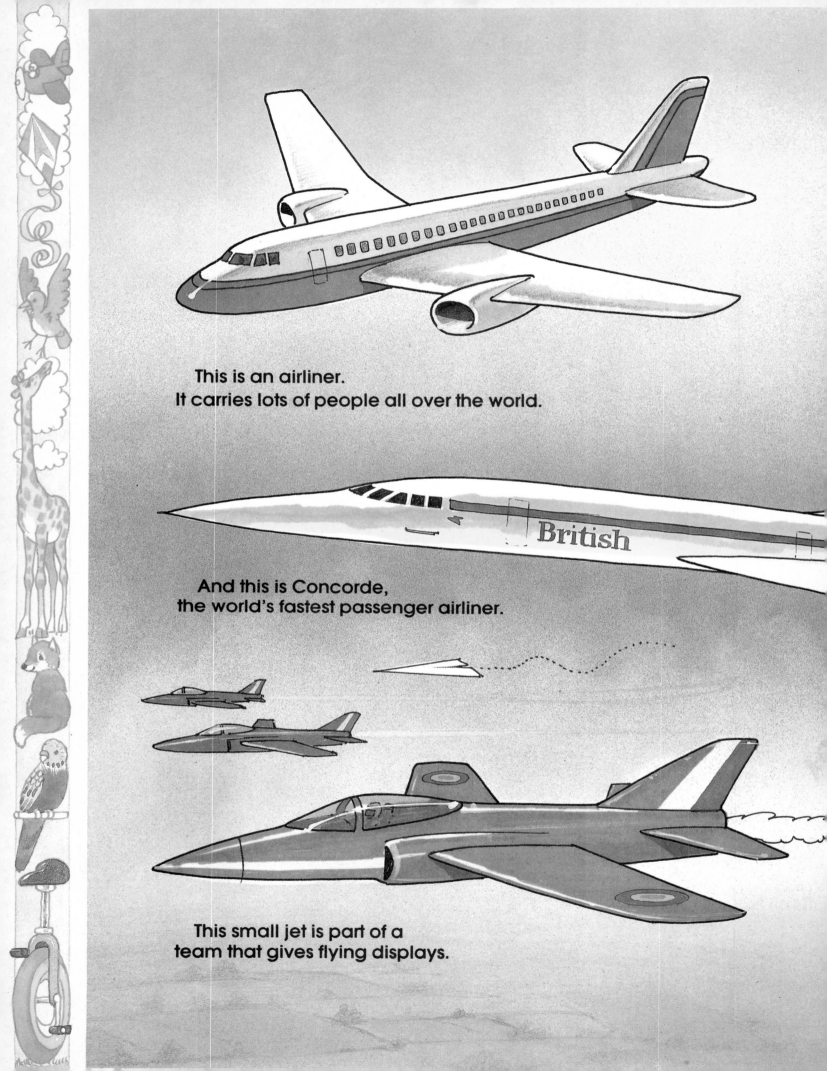

This is an airliner.
It carries lots of people all over the world.

And this is Concorde,
the world's fastest passenger airliner.

This small jet is part of a
team that gives flying displays.

This is a private plane.
It carries two people.

The helicopter
can land in
difficult places.

Here are some of the things and people you can see at an airport.

The check in.

The baggage handler.

The security check.

The waiting lounge.

The plane is being refuelled.

The baggage is being taken to the plane.

The crew arrive.

And finally, up into the air.

"What a lot of fuss, just to fly."

"If you keep going higher and higher into the air, you will reach space. There is no air in space, so you need a spacesuit."

People who go into space are called astronauts.

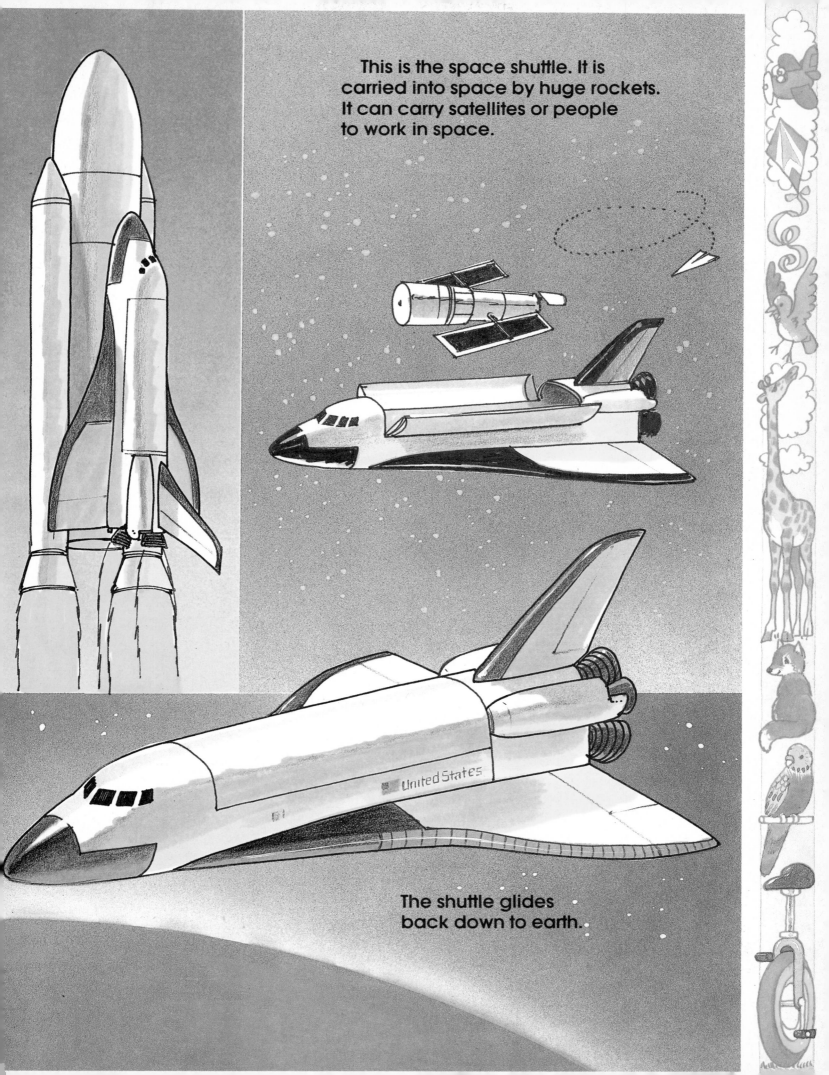

This is the space shuttle. It is
carried into space by huge rockets.
It can carry satellites or people
to work in space.

The shuttle glides
back down to earth.

"There are lots of wonderful things up in the air. But the best of all is me."

PETS

Do you have a pet?

Some people like to keep lots of pets.

If you have a very large garden you
can have pets as big as these.

If you don't have much space
small pets are just as much fun.

Here are some of the best loved pets.
Which one would you like?

Dog

Cat

Gerbil

Budgie

Tortoise

Mouse

Donkey

Pony

Rabbit

Goldfish

Guinea Pig

Hamster

Our favourite pets come in all sizes, shapes and colours. It is hard to choose just one.

Dogs

Cats

Rabbits

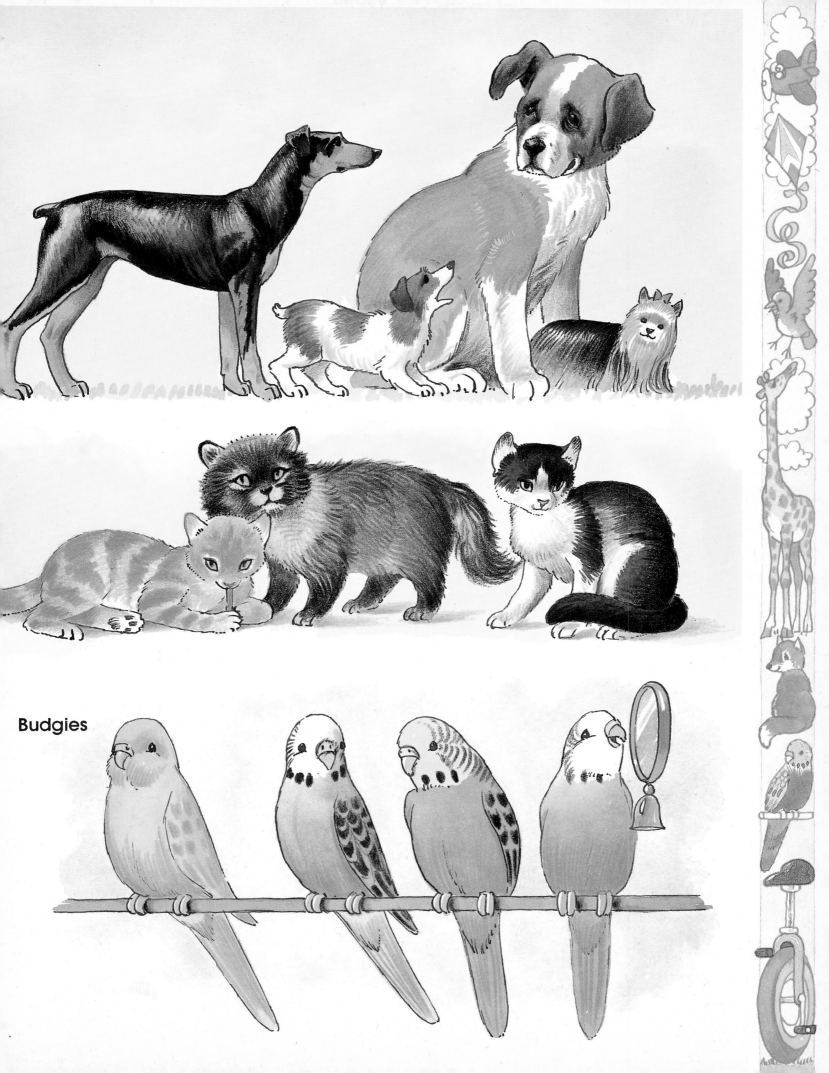

Budgies

Fish

Hamsters

Mice

Gerbils

Guinea Pigs

Shopping for your pet! You must take care to buy the right food for your pet. Some pets like a toy to play with.

TIbby

4 small tins of meat

Piece of fish

1 extra bottle of milk

New food bowl and collar

Scamp

2 large tins of meat

Dog biscuits

Chewy bone

New lead.

BUDGIE FOOD

HAMSTER GERBIL AND MOUSE MIX

Here are some pets' homes and beds. Write
the name of the pet under each one.

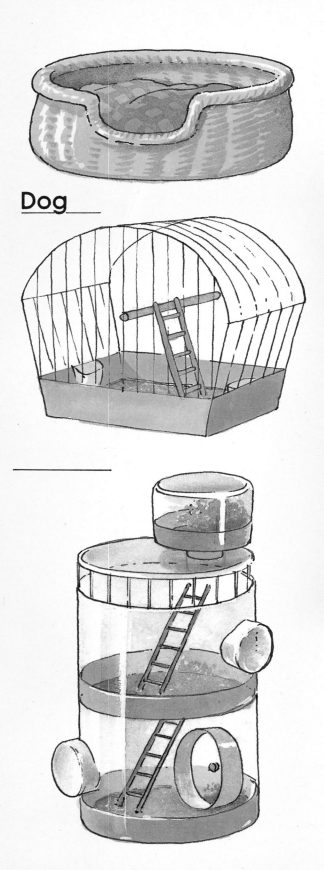

Dog

_____

Fish

Mouse

Cat

Rabbit

Guinea Pig

Dog

_____

_____

_____

Gerbil   Budgie   Hamster

Pony

If you are lucky enough to own a rabbit, or a guinea pig, it must have a proper home. On these pages you can see how to make a hutch.
You will need a grown up to help.

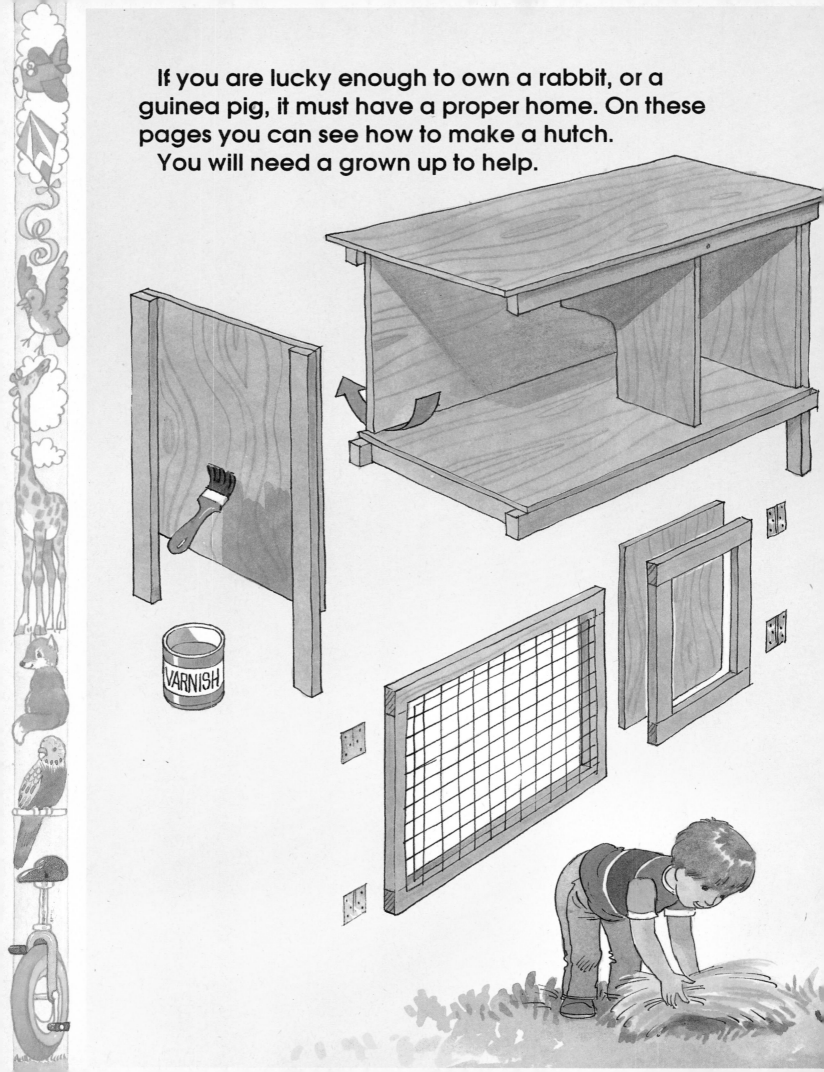

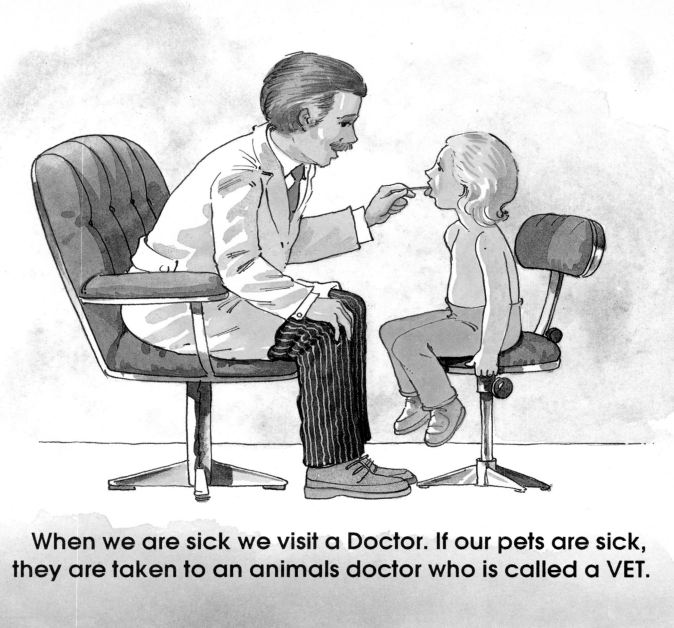

When we are sick we visit a Doctor. If our pets are sick, they are taken to an animals doctor who is called a VET.

The vet knows about all kinds of animals, and will soon make your pet well again.

If your pet has been ill, keep him warm, and quiet.

Some pets need lots of exercise, a pony needs a daily gallop.

Your dog needs a long daily walk. A goldfish just goes for a swim.

It can be great fun to enter your pet in a PET SHOW. Some must be groomed and brushed before they are judged.

You dog must be well behaved in a show.

Ponies need lots of time and hard work to get them ready for a show.

Some pets love to show off.
Others don't!

Small pets are
shown in special
cages or boxes.

Don't be sad if you don't win first time!

Puppies must be trained when they are very young. They will soon learn to 'sit', 'stay' and 'come' when they are called.

No!

Sit!

Stay!

Come!

Love and care for your pet, and you will have lots of happy times together.

VARNISH